W9-CBR-919

962495 $15.99
jFICTION LOCATED IN PICTURE BOOK SECTION
TRIPP   Tripp, Nathaniel.
           Thunderstorm!

WITHDRAWN

Freeport Public Library

314 W. Stephenson
Freeport, IL 61032
815-233-3000

Each borrower is held responsible for all materials charged on his
card and for all fines accruing on the same.

Thunderstorm!

NATHANIEL TRIPP *pictures by* JUAN WIJNGAARD

Dial Books for Young Readers *New York*

Freeport Public Library
Freeport, Illinois

Published by Dial Books for Young Readers
A Division of Penguin Books USA Inc.
375 Hudson Street
New York, New York 10014

Text copyright © 1994 by Nathaniel Tripp
Pictures copyright © 1994 by Juan Wijngaard
All rights reserved
Designed by Jane Byers Bierhorst
Printed in Hong Kong
First Edition
1 3 5 7 9 10 8 6 4 2

Library of Congress Cataloging in Publication Data

Tripp, Nathaniel
Thunderstorm! · by Nathaniel Tripp
pictures by Juan Wijngaard.—1st ed.
p. cm.
Summary · As Ben bales the freshly cut hay on
his farm and nearby animals hunt for food for their
young, the right weather conditions create a raging
thunderstorm that moves swiftly toward them.
ISBN 0-8037-1365-7 (trade)
ISBN 0-8037-1366-5 (library)
[1. Thunderstorms—Fiction. 2. Animals—Fiction. 3. Farm
life—Fiction.] I. Wijngaard, Juan, ill. II. Title.
PZ7.T73574Th 1994   [E]—dc20   93-4612   CIP   AC

The art for this book was prepared by using watercolors.
It was then color-separated and reproduced
in red, yellow, blue, and black halftones.

9628253

To Eli, Sam, and Ben, who have spent
so many hours on the porch
watching thunderstorms with me

N. T.

To my mother, who loves thunderstorms

J. W.

962495

Ben awoke at dawn. A farmer's work depends on the weather, and a long day lay ahead of him. He had to see that his freshly cut hay was dry and safely in the barn before it rained.

Other creatures were stirring as well. In the gray light outside a fox paused while crossing the pasture and watched as Ben's yellow bedroom light came on. Then she trotted down the hill looking for food for her kits.

Below the farmhouse in the hollow where a pond lay, there was a great cloud of mist showing blue-gray in the dim light. All night while the earth had gradually grown cooler, heavy cold air had gathered in that low place and the moisture in that air had formed a cloud on the ground. The fox disappeared into the mist. Almost every morning she would hunt for meadow voles by the pond's edge while the grass was still wet, softening the sound of her footsteps.

Now coffee was steaming in the farmhouse kitchen. It made its own little wisp of cloud as the lighter warm air rose from the coffee pot up over the cooler air of the kitchen. Outside the sun had begun to touch the farm with golden light. All across the land the rising sun was spreading its energy and warmth while the birds sang to the new day. The mist down by the pond disappeared almost as soon as the sunlight touched it. The fox was gone too, as though she had evaporated as well. Up in the hay meadow, spiders had spun their webs on the rows of cut hay during the night. Dew had collected on the webs when water was squeezed out of the cooling night air. Now the fragile nets sagged with the weight of it, and when the sunlight struck the beads of water, they sparkled like strings of pearls. The sky above was a hazy blue and there was not a breath of wind in the trees. The sound of

Ben in his barn, milking cows, carried far through the still air. Two deer who had come to the pond for a drink of water twitched their ears nervously at the muffled clatter of water buckets and feed pails in the barn.

There was the fox again, coming out of the woods and crossing the hay meadow with a vole in her mouth, going back to her den where her kits waited. She left footprints in a straight line in the dew-covered grass, but they didn't last for long. The warming air was soaking up water like a sponge. The glittering moisture on the cobwebs quickly faded too, drifting invisibly into the sun-warmed atmosphere. The fox paused and sniffed the air near its den on the edge of the field. There was the first whisper of a breeze, scented with pine needles and moist earth, as fresh air flowed down from the cool, wooded hillsides and out across the warming hay field.

The day before, Ben had raked the hay into spiraling rows called *windrows*. Wind blowing through the rows would dry the hay faster. Now all across the meadow the rich sweet smell of hay rose higher and higher as the sun spread its warmth. Light breezes were beginning to blow and the warmed air rose upward, carrying moisture with it. Cooler air slid down the hillsides to replace it. Insects whirled and hummed. Barn swallows swooped back and forth chasing after them.

When the fox had finished feeding her young, she came
back out of her hole under the old barbed-wire fence. The
hole was well hidden by the tangle of brush along the edge of
the field, and the entrance was protected by the strong roots of
an old pine tree. She lay down in the shade of the pine, where
nobody could see her but she could watch everything that
took place on the farm. She sniffed the air one more time,
then curled up with the tip of her tail just touching her nose.

The shadow of a hawk drifted over the field. The air above it was rising faster in the growing heat of the day, just as warm smoke from a campfire does. The hawk steered into the rising air and was carried upward with it, soaring higher and higher, not needing to move its wings. The bird watched the field below to see if its shadow might startle a mouse into view as it passed across the field. The hawk, hundreds of feet above the farm, could also see Ben leaving the barn; watched the cows as they wandered out to the high pasture; and looked down on Ben's wife Emma as she went out to the vegetable garden to pick some fresh peas. Elsewhere, over other fields or beside mountain cliffs where warm air was also rising, other hawks were circling, being lifted by the wind.

Far above the hawks, five miles up, where the air is so cold at twenty degrees below zero, it would freeze a bird solid, a jet airliner was crossing from east to west, as it did every morning at this time. Warm and snug inside their cocoon of metal and plastic, the passengers looked down on the patchwork of fields and forests far below while their breakfast was served. Only a few clouds lay scattered over the landscape. But up in the airliner's cockpit the pilot could see a line of big clouds climbing high into the sky ahead. This was the cold front that

he had seen on his weather maps before the flight began. The clouds marked the leading edge of cool, fresh, heavy air sweeping down from Canada. This heavy air acted like a wedge as it moved toward the southeast, driving in underneath the lighter, warm moist air and lifting it upward even faster and more powerfully than the sun's heat could. The passengers in the airplane could even feel a gentle "bump" when the airplane entered the clouds and was lifted up as it crossed over the cold front.

Twenty-two thousand miles above the airplane a man-made satellite was watching the earth with one glass eye. It was taking pictures of the cold front, and the swirls and lines of clouds that marked other weather systems across the land and seas far below. The satellite sent the pictures back to earth by radio, four pictures every hour. Then the pictures were copied and sent out to weather forecasters at airports and television stations.

Almost a hundred million miles farther away the sun was burning as fiercely as always, sending its energy toward the earth. The heat from the sun was making the air move all around the world, not just over Ben's fields. As the day went on, air heated by the sun was rising higher and faster. Over the farm the dew that had made the cobwebs sparkle and had shown the fox's morning footprints, now rose invisibly along with the scent of the hay. The hawk continued to circle in and out of the columns of air, feeling their heat and lift. But the air kept pushing much higher, far beyond the hawk. About a mile and a half above the farm, where the rising air began to enter much colder air, a funny thing began to happen. A cloud began to form. At first it was just a small cloud, with a flat bottom and a puffy white top. It formed for the same reason that the mist had formed overnight down by the pond, and that a person's breath shows like steam on a cold winter day. When air is chilled, it can't hold as much invisible moisture as it can when it is warm. The moisture in the air forms tiny droplets of water. The droplets are so small that they still float in the air, but we can see them now as a cloud, or mist, or steam.

Weather forecasters could see the clouds forming on the latest satellite photographs. They knew that the sun's energy would make the clouds get bigger as the day went on, and add to the lifting power of the cold front. They decided to forecast strong thunderstorms for later in the afternoon. Emma heard the forecast on the radio while she was in the kitchen shelling peas. It had been a very hot and dry summer, and the rain and cooler air brought by a storm would be welcome. But not before the hay crop was in the barn.

Ben could tell the storm was coming. He had been watching the sky while he worked. Now he drove the tractor around the hay field in big circles, pulling a hay rake. The rake turned the windrows over so the undersides would dry. A flock of barn swallows began to gather in the air behind Ben. They had

learned that the hay rake stirred up a lot of insects. The birds darted back and forth, scooping insects from the air, while the clouds above them grew larger and larger, and the hawk slowly circled lower, watching to see if the rake would uncover a mouse.

Everything was humming in the midday heat. Bees zipped back and forth gathering pollen from wildflowers. The swallows swooped into the big, dark barn whenever they had a mouthful of bugs for their young. At the pond bullfrogs, with their big black-and-gold eyes, were watching for insects too. Gusts of wind made the pond surface ripple.

The air was steadily moving as the lifting power of the sun grew stronger. The clouds that had formed over the hay meadow drifted past the farm. Some were much bigger than others, their tops billowing high into the sky. These mushrooming clouds had a power of their own now. Their tops had grown so tall that they were sucking up the warm wet air near the ground and adding it to their mass. Like giant snails feeding on the sun-warmed air, they grew steadily larger as they crawled across the sky.

Before long, showers began to fall in scattered places ahead of the cold front. These were isolated spots where the clouds had drawn their moisture especially high into the air. But while showers were falling on the ground from these clouds, there were snowstorms inside the high cloud tops! The moisture up there was freezing and gathering together into snow and ice pellets. Then, as these got heavy enough to fall down toward the ground, the warmer air below melted them into raindrops. As he finished raking his hay, Ben could see that there were showers falling here and there across the distant hills. Some of the tallest clouds had gray streaks hanging from them. He hurriedly towed the rake back to the equipment shed, calling to Emma and asking her to make him a sandwich as he drove past the farmhouse. There wasn't time for him to sit down for lunch.

As soon as Ben left, the fox got up and trotted out into the field. Perhaps the rake had uncovered something for her own lunch. She sniffed the freshly turned hay, poking her sharp nose into it here and there as she walked around. Now and then she would stand perfectly still and listen for the slightest rustle or squeak. Then suddenly the hawk swooped down and pounced on a mouse that was just a little distance in front of the fox. She ran toward the hawk, but with a powerful thrust

of its wings it leapt back in the air again, the mouse firmly
gripped in its talons. Then the fox froze. She could hear the
tractor coming back again. She started back toward the den,
always keeping just out of sight. On the way she noticed a big
black beetle crawling through the grass. She pounced on the
beetle, flipped it into the air with the tip of her nose, then
caught it in her mouth. Not a great lunch, but better than
nothing.

Now Ben was ready to start baling his hay. The *baler* is a big machine towed by the tractor that gathers the loose hay and packs it into tight squares tied with strings. The bales of hay pop out the back of the baler onto a wagon that trails along behind. Ben nervously looked at the sky again as he started to bale. Showers here, showers there, but luckily no showers overhead so far. He steered the tractor with one hand and ate his sandwich with the other. The tractor's diesel engine roared, the baler thumped and clattered. Sweat rolled down Ben's face as he worked in the hot, humid air. One by one the tight green bales of hay began to pile up on the wagon.

Meanwhile, just a hundred miles west of the farm, something new was happening along the approaching cold front. Inside some of the clouds the warm air was rising so swiftly that no rain was able to fall. The winds inside these clouds, blowing straight up at fifty miles an hour, kept pushing the snow and ice pellets higher and higher into the sky. This wind also drew in even more hot, wet air at the bottom. The energy of the sun and the powerful wedge of the cold front was keeping millions of tons of water suspended inside some of these clouds. Scientists call clouds like this *cells*, and they seem to have a life of their own.

But the clouds that had become cells contained more than just wind and water. They were beginning to carry electrical

charges as well. People still don't know exactly how it happens, but it seems that the swirling of ice and snow inside the cloud generates electricity just as people can create electricity when they shuffle across a rug on a cold winter day. The storm cells were like huge batteries, charged by the upward swirling wind inside them. There were no sparks yet; the clouds were still silent. But with the electricity building up, and all that water suspended in the sky, they seemed about to explode.

Ben could see these clouds when they were still far away. Their tops had risen so high—five or six miles—that they had spread out into the thinner air up there like wide, flat hats. They are called *anvil clouds*, because they are shaped like a blacksmith's anvil.

The sun was shining brightly, but there were lots of anvil clouds coming closer when some of Ben's neighbors began arriving at the farm to help him get the hay in the barn. They knew Ben's crop was in danger and wanted to help out. Now the first rumbles of thunder could be heard deep within the clouds of the cold front. The thunder was a signal from inside each cell that it had stopped growing taller and had become "active."

The active phase of the cell would begin when the winds

rushing upward could no longer keep the great weight of ice
and water up in the air. Sometimes there can be enough water
to fill fifty thousand swimming pools, suspended in the air by
a big, strong cell; when that water finally begins to fall, it
carries a lot of cold air down with it. When the rush of cold
air that falls with the rain hits the ground and spreads out, it
chokes off the supply of warm air that was rising up through
the cell's center. The cell then falls apart and the thunderstorm
is over if there are no new cells nearby.

On this hot summer day there were lots of cells, and the rising and falling of wind and water inside them wasn't the only thing happening there. As the first drops of rain began to fall, the electricity that had been building up inside the cells began to jump back and forth in the giant sparks we call lightning. Most of the time these sparks would just jump between different parts of the cloud, but often they would also strike the ground below. They were triggered by the up-and-down movement of air and water inside the cell, because now winds were blowing straight down around the outside, carrying ice and water, while the warm winds were still blowing straight up through the center, like smoke going up a

chimney. The falling winds can often go as fast as seventy miles an hour, right past the rising winds, which are still going fifty miles an hour. Along with generating lightning this difference in wind speed and direction, called *wind shear*, can tear the wings right off an airplane unlucky enough to be caught in it. Of course raindrops are often caught in it. Falling in the downdraft they may drift over into the updraft and get sent soaring back up to the top of the cloud again where they will freeze and become coated with a second layer of ice. When they fall a second time, they are much bigger and heavier, but they may still be caught in the updraft again and again.

When they finally reach the ground, they are too big to have melted and they are called hailstones. You can cut hailstones open and count the rings of clear ice to see how many times they have traveled to the top of the cell. Imagine a wind strong enough to blow ice cubes straight up! Imagine so huge an amount of water that it would take a freight train five hundred miles long to haul it, all being churned and swirled inside a thunderstorm. The electricity generated by a large cell is about the same amount as is used by a small town. Some big sparks are made inside such a storm. Many of these lightning bolts are five miles long. They are only as thick as a pencil, but they are hotter than the surface of the sun, and the electricity travels at the speed of light. The moist air surrounding a lightning bolt explodes with a sound as loud as a cannon. Thunder sounds the way it does because the sound follows the shape of the lightning bolt. The "boom" of a cannon just comes from one spot. The "boom" of exploding air around a lightning bolt is miles long and filled with twists and turns. Also, it echoes off other clouds and the ground below, ending up as the rumbling sound we know as thunder. After each lightning bolt an active cell needs only about twenty seconds to recharge itself, just like a giant battery. Then it is ready to produce another one.

Ben couldn't hear the thunder above the sound of his farm machinery. But he looked up when the farm suddenly fell under the shadow cast by the giant storm clouds. They covered the sky in the west, and he could see churning inside as the shafts of sunlight shifted back and forth against the cloud top. Most of his hay was baled, and his neighbors were quickly loading it in the barn. Ben decided it would be too dangerous to keep working in the open field as the storm steadily drew closer. Lightning is attracted toward things that stand up higher than the rest of the landscape, and a farmer on a tractor would be just such a thing. The small amount of hay that still remained in a corner of the field was not worth the risk. So he shut off the tractor's engine and got down to unhitch the baler.

The air above the farm was strangely still. The surface of the pond reflected the approaching storm like a mirror. But even

the animals seemed to sense that something big was coming. The swallows stopped chasing insects and lined up on the telephone wires near their nests, and the hawk landed in a tree and huddled close to the trunk. The fox yawned and stretched nervously, then went down into her den to be with her kits. Now with all the machinery turned off, the almost constant rumble of thunder sounded like the drums of an approaching army. Ben started his tractor again and began hauling the last wagon loaded with hay down to the barn, where his neighbors were hard at work. One man and his son were throwing the bales off another wagon and onto a clattering conveyor belt. The conveyor lifted the bales high up into the barn loft, where another man and Ben's wife were busily stashing the bales away. Then there was an especially loud explosion of thunder, and everyone began to work twice as hard.

All along the stormy front new cells were being born while old ones were dying nearby. The tall clouds headed toward the farm were made of clusters of several cells; some were still growing, some were active, and some were fading away. There was hardly any pause between the flashes of lightning. The sky to the west was almost green now, with pink flickers of electricity behind a curtain of rain and hail.

Ben knew that by counting the seconds between a flash of lightning and the sound of its thunder, it was easy to tell how far away the lightning was. Sound takes five seconds to travel a mile. The air above the farm was still nearly motionless, yet there was a distant rushing sound between the rolls of thunder. It was the sound of air and ice swirling inside the approaching clouds.

Finally all the bales were in the loft, and the workers
shouted to each other as they swung the heavy barn doors
shut. "Tie the doors closed!" "Put the car windows up!" Five
miles, four miles, three miles…the distance to the lightning
grew shorter and shorter, the time between flashes and the
roll of thunder less and less, and everyone took shelter inside
the farmhouse.

Ben's cows, which up to now had seemed to take no notice
of the approaching storm, suddenly began to run across the
high pasture toward the shelter of some woods. The first gusts
of wind began to sweep through the treetops.

Trees suddenly began to wave back and forth and thrash about as the leading edge of the falling cold air came sweeping through. Almost immediately there was a brilliant flash of lightning and a sharp crack of thunder. Then the trees disappeared behind a curtain of silvery rain and hail. Next the downdraft hit the farmhouse, and everyone inside could feel the building shake. Immediately the air felt much colder. It even smelled different than the air that had been lingering close to the ground. Then hail began to pound on the metal farmhouse roof, rattling down the eaves and bouncing on the lawn.

The fox curled up around her babies inside their warm, dry tunnel in the earth. The swallows snuggled down atop their nests in the barn. Other wild birds huddled deep within the protective branches of trees to avoid being struck by hailstones or swept away by the winds. And the winds seemed to be gusting harder by the moment, carrying their great load of ice and water down, then spreading out from the base of the cell as they neared the ground. The woods looked like a storm-tossed sea, as wave after wave of wind passed through them. The air was filled with green leaves and bits of branches torn loose by the wind and hail. Now and then a weak-rooted tree would topple over, or a big limb would crash to the ground. But the sound was lost in the roar of the storm.

The old pine tree growing above the fox's den swayed in the wind. Its roots had reached around the den itself and went deep into the ground. Its top stood high in the air. Many years ago when the tree was quite small, Ben's grandfather had built a barbed-wire fence along this side of the hay meadow. He had nailed the wire to this pine, using it as a living fence post. Over the years as the pine grew, it surrounded the wires and buried them deep within its wood. Now there was a shuddering there, and even the fox felt it. The hair on the back of her neck stood straight up as a highly charged part of a storm cell passed right overhead. In the instant that followed, a great surge of electricity leapt through the pine tree. Moisture inside the tree was turned to steam along the lightning's path, and one side of the tree exploded, sending huge long splinters of yellow wood flying out across the field. But instead of continuing down through the tree's roots and around the den where the fox family lay, the lightning chose another path. It went into the barbed wire, followed the old fence for hundreds of feet, then disappeared down a fence post into low, wet ground. All along the lightning's course through the fence the wire itself instantly melted, sprinkling droplets of white hot iron along the ground. The boom of the bolt's thunder sounded and resounded off the hills and the cloud towers, retracing the lightning's path through the sky, and the fox family huddled even closer together.

The hail ended as the cell's center passed by. A steady rain fell now, quickly extinguishing the little fires started by the bits of melted barbed wire. In the barn the big hewn timbers creaked and moaned as another gust of wind hit, but this old barn had seen a hundred storms as bad as this before. Warm and snug inside its dark cavern the families of swallows chittered to each other, waiting for the storm to end. The scent of the freshly harvested hay filled the air. Soon the shaking gusts of wind came less often, then not at all. There was just the steady beat of rain on the roof. The time between a lightning flash and the roll of its thunder grew longer and longer as the cells moved eastward, away from the farm.

The sun came out for a moment, shining through cool, clear air against the gray backside of the storm. Raindrops falling just east of the farm broke the sunlight into all its separate colors, making a rainbow that arched over the landscape, glowing brightly against the dark wall of retreating clouds. Now the only sound was the rush of water in a dozen little streams and rivulets. Everything was clean and refreshed, and there was a tingling smell in the air. This was the smell of nitric acid, which lightning creates in small amounts as it explodes through the air. It is a natural fertilizer, and all green things would grow a little faster over the next few days as the water and fertilizer soaked into the soil.

There would also be some extra work for Ben to do:
branches to be picked up and tossed aside, and a fence line
was in need of repair. But at this moment as the sun set, the
world seemed reborn. The fox came out of her den and sniffed
at the strange splinters of wood littering the ground nearby.
Her kits emerged too, and started chasing each other and
rolling in the wet grass, unaware of the close call they'd had.

The hawk ruffled its feathers so they would dry faster, and began to doze off on its perch while the swallows went out for one last happy swirling flight of the evening.

Shadows lengthened until they covered everything, and the color of the sky faded to darkness. Down by the pond the bullfrogs began to call to each other, and as cold air slipped down from the hillsides, a pool of mist began to form.

About the Author

Nathaniel Tripp has written about meteorology for a number of publications. A part-time farmer, he has also written and produced television projects about science, nature, and technology. Mr. Tripp, who was born in New York City, now lives with his family in St. Johnsbury, Vermont.

About the Artist

Juan Wijngaard studied art at the Royal College of Art in England and has won several major awards for his illustrations, including the 1985 Kate Greenaway Medal for *Sir Gawain and the Loathly Lady*. His first book published by Dial, *Going to Sleep on the Farm*, was called "captivating" by *Kirkus Reviews* and was given a starred review by *Booklist*. Mr. Wijngaard now lives in Santa Monica, California, with his wife and son.